Christopher Columbus

A Hands-on-History Look at the Life and Adventures of Explorer Christopher Columbus

Written by Mary Tucker

Illustrated by Judy Hierstein

Teaching & Learning Company

1204 Buchanan St., P.O. Box 10
Carthage, IL 62321-0010

This book belongs to

Cover art by Judy Hierstein

Copyright © 2002, Teaching & Learning Company

ISBN No. 1-57310-328-4

Printing No. 987654321

Teaching & Learning Company
1204 Buchanan St., P.O. Box 10
Carthage, IL 62321-0010

Table of Contents

Dear Teacher or Parent,

Christopher Columbus used to be the hero of our history books, but lately he's had some "bad press" and is sometimes even laughed at. That's nothing new for Columbus; he went through the same kind of thing before and after his voyages to the new world. It's true that he didn't find what he was looking for, but he made some amazing discoveries and cleared the way for other explorers to venture across the wide Western Ocean. He is an important historical figure with whom first through fourth graders should be familiar. And, as it turns out, his life was exciting and full of adventure—a fun study for anybody!

Your students will enjoy learning some interesting facts about Columbus that are not common knowledge. Through the activities in this book, students will discover what it was like to sail a small ship across a large ocean, and they'll get a chance to see firsthand how a compass works and how they can put it to practical use. Students will be able to consider Columbus' voyage to the New World from his crew's point of view, play some fun games that replicate Columbus' experiences and even make a paper version of the *Santa María* to float.

In addition, students will learn much more about world geography as they use a map or globe to see where Columbus went and note how far it was from where he started (not to mention how far it was from where he intended to be). They will be challenged to imagine how they would have felt so far from home and familiar things.

The study ends with an action rhyme/skit for students to perform that summarizes this study. After learning about Columbus' dreams and mistakes and accomplishments, they'll understand the value of his contribution to history and even begin to see his effect on their lives today.

Sincerely,

Mary

Mary Tucker

Christopher Columbus

Resources

To enhance this study for your students, the following resources are recommended:

Books to Read Aloud

Christopher Columbus by Jan Gleiter and Kathleen Thompson (Raintree Publishers, 1987)

Meet Christopher Columbus by James T. de Kay (Random House, 1989)

The Swiss Family Robinson by Johann Wyss (Random House, 1999)

Where Do You Think You're Going, Christopher Columbus? by Jean Fritz (G.P. Putnam's Sons, 1980)

Videos

Christopher Columbus Video and Activity Book (an animated video) For more information about this video, go to the NestFamily web site at:
www1.nestentertainment.com/store/product
Click on "animated hero classics."

The Swiss Family Robinson (Walt Disney Studios, 1960)

Web Sites

www.mariner.org/age/columbus.html
This site provides pictures and interesting information about Columbus including maps showing the routes of his voyages.

www1.minn.net/~keithp/index.htm
At the Columbus Navigation Homepage, your students can see pictures and discover interesting facts about the three ships Columbus took on his first voyage as well as explanations of various types of navigation and navigational tools used in that time.

www.shipsofdiscovery.org/columbus.htm
Students will enjoy this web site about recent efforts to find nine of Columbus' ships that sank during his four voyages.

www.castellobanfi.com/features/story_3.html
What food did Columbus and his crew eat while sailing across the ocean, and what foods did they discover when they landed at their destinations? Your students will enjoy finding out this interesting information about eating in the 15th century.

Christopher Columbus

A Boy Named Christopher

The city of Genoa was on the west coast of Italy, and its harbor was always filled with ships. Sailors and traders from all over the world were a common sight on its streets. It was in this sailing town that Christopher Columbus was born in 1451. Though he was not born into a seaman's family (his father was a weaver and cloth merchant) Christopher quickly grew to love sailing. He once said that sailing makes a person wish to learn the secrets of the world. Everyone in town got used to seeing the red-haired boy squinting his eyes, looking out across the sea as if he could see the distant lands where he longed to sail.

He and two of his younger brothers had a small boat that they sailed in the Bay of Genoa. They often sailed to little islands in the bay and camped out overnight, spending their time fishing and swimming, and racing other boats back to the docks.

Chris heard stories about fabulous riches in a place called the Indies far away to the east. While he worked for his father making cloth, the boy dreamed of sailing to new lands and having adventures. Chris' job was to card wool by running a rough comb through it to get out the impurities. But he hoped someday to be a sailor. When he had the time, he sat quietly under the window of a nearby wine shop, listening to the sea tales of sailors inside.

Since he was needed to work in his father's shop, Christopher only went to school for a few hours a day, learning the basics of reading, writing and arithmetic. His father taught him how to be a business man. When Christopher was 14 years old, he went with his father on a voyage to buy wool. They sailed for several days along the coasts of Italy and France. That must have been an exciting trip for the young would-be sailor. After that trip, Chris' father often let him go along on the trading expeditions. Perhaps in this way the boy began to learn how to be a true seaman. He noticed the changing colors of the sea and the patterns of the wind and currents. He closely watched the sailors handle the rigging, weigh the anchor and steer.

Map Activity

Have students find Italy, then the city of Genoa, on a world map or globe. Ask them what sea Christopher Columbus would have sailed on as a boy. (Ligurian Sea) What bigger sea did this lead into? (Mediterranean Sea)

Talking About Boats

Ask how many students have taken boat rides. Let volunteers share their experiences.

Talk about the fun of riding in a boat. Discuss the various kinds of boats one can travel in today. See how many students can think of (canoe, raft, kayak, rowboat, motorboat, sailboat, houseboat, paddleboat, yacht, tugboat, barge, cruise ship, aircraft carrier, submarine, to name a few). Talk about each kind of boat to make sure students understand the purpose of each and the way it is moved across the water.

Then ask each student to say which boat he or she would like to travel in and explain why. Where would they go? Who would they take with them? Would they work on the boat or just enjoy the ride and let someone else do all the work? How long would they want to be gone?

Action Song

Have children sing this song and do the actions, pretending to be Christopher Columbus.

Sailing Song

To the tune of "My Bonnie Lies over the Ocean"

I wonder what's over the ocean.
(Lean forward to the left as you shade eyes with hand and look far away.)

I wonder what's over the sea.
(Lean forward to the right as you shade eyes with hand and look far away.)

Someday I'll sail over the ocean
(Move hand in wavey motion.)

That will be an adventure for me!
(Jump up and raise hands over head.)

Sailing, sailing,
(Move hand in wavey motion.)

In a ship over the sea, the sea.
(Point forward.)

Sailing, sailing,
(Move hand in wavey motion.)

That will be an adventure for me!
(Jump up and raise hands over head.)

Explorers Exploring

As Columbus was growing up, many explorers were searching for a direct, safe route to the East. The East Indies (Asia, especially China) was rich in gold, precious stones, silk and exotic spices. The spices were especially wanted because meat often spoiled in those days of no refrigeration. Spices made the meat taste better and flavored other food as well.

Traders had been bringing these popular items from the East for some time on overland trade routes to the city of Constantinople where they could be shipped to various European ports. But when the Turks invaded Constantinople in 1453, renaming it Istanbul, they cut off much of this trade. There was big money to be made for the country that could find a quick and easy way to get the Asian products to Europe. Portuguese sailors hoped to reach the East Indies by sailing around Africa, but no one knew for sure how far south Africa extended or even if it was possible to go around it! Some people believed that getting too close to the equator would be dangerous. Would they be burned to death in fiery waters? Could anyone live that close to the equator?

In spite of the difficulties and possible dangers, King Alfonso V of Portugal encouraged further exploration of a trade route. He hoped to pay off his debts with profits from the discoveries and trade. So Portuguese sailors relentlessly sailed various distances around Africa until Vasco de Gama sailed around the tip of Africa and made it all the way to India near the end of the 15th century. Unfortunately, during these voyages of exploration, the Portuguese stopped at many points along the way and captured Africans, later selling them for slaves. Slave trading became a big business.

Map Activity

Have students find China on a map or globe. Then have someone point out Africa. Ask students if they think going around Africa would have been the best way to get to the East from Italy or Portugal. Were there any other possible ways to get there?

Have students point out Istanbul on the map or globe. Note its distance from China. Why would bringing things back from the East to Europe be better by ship than by land?

Christopher Columbus

A Sea Battle

By the time Christopher Columbus was 25 years old he had sailed all over the Mediterranean Sea. He had traveled to France, Africa and Greece and had many adventures. His life's wish had come true–he was a sailor. Then in 1476 Christopher heard some exciting news. Five ships were going to leave Genoa and sail to England! That was farther than he had ever been, far from the Mediterranean Sea. He immediately applied for work on one of the ships, and in the spring he sailed off on his greatest adventure yet.

One day a sailor stationed high on a mast began shouting and pointing at some ships in the distance. They were warships! As they came closer to Christopher's ship, they began shooting at it! Cannonballs crashed into the side; ropes and sails were torn to shreds; masts were knocked down. Christopher's ship shot back at the warships. Noise and smoke and the screams of injured and dying sailors filled the air all day. Many were killed, and Christopher was injured. When the ship began to sink, he jumped into the sea. Fortunately, a wooden oar was floating nearby and he grabbed it. He was in the water for hours before he reached land late at night. As Christopher dragged himself up on the beach, some men came down to help him. They told him that he was in Portugal.

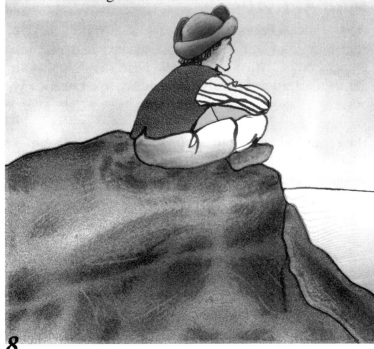

Map Activity

Have students find Portugal on a map or globe. Ask them what ocean Christopher was in when he got to Portugal. Back then it was called the great Western Ocean.

Action Rhyme

Divide students into two groups and have them stand in two straight lines facing each other. Have them do the actions as they say this fun action rhyme.

Group 1: When I was just a little boy my father was a weaver.

Group 2: Weave, weave, weave some more. Weaving all day is a bore!

(Both groups weave in, out and around one another, looking bored.)

Group 1: I didn't like the work at all because I had sea fever!

Group 2: Swaying, swaying with the waves is the way to spend your days!

(All students sway back and forth toward one another, looking happy.)

Group 1: One day I got aboard a ship sailing far away.

Group 2: Sailing, sailing on the sea. This is just the life for me!

(All students move slowly up and down, undulating their bodies as if on the sea.)

Group 1: Suddenly we were attacked! What an awful day.

Group 2: Crashing, splashing all around. See, the ship is going down.

(Students smack their hands together and wobble as if unsteady.)

Group 1: To save my life I jumped out of the ship into the sea.

Group 2: Swim, swim with all my might! Keep on swimming through the night.

(Students move their arms in swimming motions as they move around the room.)

Group 1: I grabbed an oar and swam away. The water had saved me.

Group 2: Swim, swim and swim some more till I finally reach the shore.

(Students "swim" to one side of the room, then raise arms in triumph.)

Christopher Columbus

At Home in Portugal

Christopher Columbus decided to stay in Portugal. In fact, he lived there off and on for about nine years near the busy seaport town of Lisbon. While there, he got married and had a son. He continued to sail as often as he could and when he was home, he spent much of his time talking with other sailors about the lands they had seen. He also helped run a store that sold maps.

As he listened to sailors talking about the need for a good route to the Indies, Columbus decided he was going to beat everyone else there! He didn't think sailing around Africa was the best way. So far no ship had been able to get around the whole continent. In fact, no one even knew where Africa ended. Columbus had another idea. Why not take a shortcut and sail west straight across the Western Ocean? He knew the world was round, so he was sure he could get to the East by going the opposite direction.

He studied maps and books, especially a book called *The Adventures of Marco Polo.* Long before Columbus had been born, Marco Polo had traveled to the East. He had gone by land, traveling over deserts and mountains. Polo's adventures inspired Columbus and made him determined to be the first one to take a ship to China.

The biggest problem with his plan was the great Western Ocean. Nobody knew how big it was. Nobody really knew anything about it. Some people said it would take three years to cross the ocean. And how would he get back? People believed that if the world was round, then going west meant going downhill! How could Columbus sail back home uphill? However, one book he read said that a person could walk around the whole world in only about four and a half years. Surely Columbus could sail to the Indies in much less time, no more than a month or so. An ancient Greek philosopher had written that the ocean was quite small. This seemed reasonable since surely there was more land than water on the Earth.

Another of the books Columbus read was written by an Englishman named Sir John Mandeville. He claimed to have traveled to the Indies and to have seen men with feet like umbrellas, people whose eyes were on their shoulders and ants that dug for gold! Actually, Mandeville had never been to the Indies; he made it all up. But many people, like Columbus, believed his stories. (Somewhat like some people today believe stories of strange creatures on other planets.)

In 1484 Columbus went to see King John, the ruler of Portugal. Christopher Columbus was 33 years old, tall and well built, and not a bit shy. He told the king that he knew he could find the Indies by sailing west and he promised to bring back gold. King John decided that Columbus was just a big talker. He didn't believe he could do what he said. "No," said the king. "We'll continue pursuing the African route." Columbus was crushed, but not ready to give up.

Creature Features Art Activity

Hand out art paper and colored markers, crayons or paints and paintbrushes. Have students create the strange creatures Columbus believed might be found in the Indies or make up their own creatures.

When the students are done, have them hold up their creatures and tell about them, including some of their strange habits and ways of life.

Christopher Columbus

It's a Small, Small World

One of Columbus' miscalculations in his plan to reach the Indies was the size of the Earth. At that time most educated people agreed that the Earth was round and many maps were drawn of it. However, none of the people who drew the maps had ever been around the world! They used their own calculations to decide on the Earth's size. Columbus spent a lot of time reading what ancient scholars such as Ptolemy had written about the world. Ptolemy believed the Earth to be half the size it actually was. Columbus figured that the distance by ocean from Europe to the Indies was farther than Ptolemy said but much shorter than most people of his day believed. He thought the distance around the whole Earth was probably about 20,000 miles. He wasn't as far off as you might think. The actual number is 25,000 miles.

A cosmographer named Toscanelli sent Columbus a copy of his hand-drawn chart of the distance between Europe and the East Indies. According to the chart, there were no continents between them. Toscanelli and Columbus had no idea of the North and South American continents that should have appeared in the center of the chart.

Christopher Columbus was convinced his ideas were right, and he began devoting all his time and energy to the voyage he would make one day to the East Indies. He called it the Enterprise of the Indies.

Making a Map

Before involving students in this activity, remove all world maps and globes from view. Give each student a copy of page 11. Talk about Toscanelli's chart at the top of the page. Then challenge students to draw a correct map of the area between Europe and China. When they are done, compare their ideas to a world map to see how close they came. Point out that they have much more knowledge of the world than Columbus had. Understanding this makes Columbus' voyages even more remarkable.

Discussion & Song

Talk about how much "smaller" the world seems today because we know so much more about people and places far away. Ask students why we know so much more about one another today.

Point out that knowing about the people who live in other parts of the world helps us not be afraid of them or prejudiced against them. If possible, sing the popular Disney song, "It's a Small World" or play the song on a tape or CD.

Off to Spain

King John of Portugal had refused to pay for Columbus' voyage to the Indies, apparently because he didn't believe Columbus knew what he was talking about. However, after refusing Columbus, the king sent a secret mission of men to try out Columbus' ideas for getting to the Indies. The mission failed because the sailors were not experienced enough on the high seas. A bad storm forced them to return without accomplishing anything.

Columbus was furious when he found out, and he decided to leave Portugal. His wife had died and he was in debt, so it seemed a good time to go to Spain. With almost no money and nowhere to go once they reached Spain, Columbus and his son went to a monastery where kindhearted monks welcomed and encouraged them. When Columbus decided to go talk to the king and queen, he left his son at the monastery to be educated.

Name _____

Making a Map

This is what Toscanelli thought Columbus would see on his voyage to the East Indies. What is missing? Draw your own map below to show what was really across the ocean between Europe and the East (China).

King Ferdinand & Queen Isabella

Christopher Columbus went to see the king and queen of Spain, but they were too busy to see him. It took a whole year before the queen agreed to see him. Even then she didn't agree to Columbus' plan for going to the Indies. "Wait," she told him. So he waited for more weeks and months. While he waited he talked about his Enterprise of the Indies, but many people laughed at his ideas.

After two years of waiting, Columbus decided he might as well go back to Portugal. Maybe he could change King John's mind. But when he got to Portugal, everyone was celebrating explorer Bartholomew Diaz's trip around Africa. King John couldn't be bothered with Columbus' crazy ideas. Columbus went back to Spain and waited another three years before Queen Isabella invited Columbus to come and see her. Finally the queen agreed to get him the ships he needed and finance his voyage across the Western Ocean to the Indies.

"What prize do you want if you are successful?" Queen Isabella asked Columbus. He replied that he wanted gold, silver and pearls. He also wanted to be called Admiral of the Ocean Sea (another name for the Western Ocean), and he wanted to be the governor of all the lands he discovered. The queen would not agree to all of this, but she finally changed her mind and Christopher Columbus' great adventure began.

Getting Ready

The three ships Columbus needed would be made ready at the harbor town of Palos. However, in those days the term *ship* was given only to the flagship, the *Santa María*. It was larger and stronger than the other two, the *Niña* and the *Pinta*. These two were called "caravels." Even the *Santa María* was not very big, only about 70 to 78 feet long. This meant that the 40 men and boys who would serve on the wooden ship would be crowded. They would have to sleep in shifts because there just wasn't enough space for all of them to bed down at the same time.

Columbus would command the larger ship, the *Santa María*. A seaman named Vicente Pinzon would take charge of the *Niña* while his brother Martin commanded the *Pinta*. From their first meeting, the two brothers and Columbus did not like one another. However, the Pinzon brothers were well respected in the area and men began signing up to join the expedition immediately. There were seamen, a surgeon, carpenters, a silversmith, a language interpreter, servants of the king and queen, the man who owned the *Santa María*, some boys who had never been to sea before and four criminals who had been pardoned by the Spanish court so they could join the crew. The men on the three ships totaled 90 and all but four were Spanish. One was Portuguese and three, including Columbus, were Italians.

A Ship to Sail

Copy the double ship pattern on page 13 on heavy paper and give one to each student. (To make the ships more durable, laminate the pattern sheets, front and back after students color them.) Have them color it and cut it out, leaving the two ships connected at the top. Then show them how to glue a floatable object (wood, Styrofoam™, a plastic pill bottle with the top on it or an empty film canister) between the two patterns. Then tape the patterns together at the front and back. Provide a container of water where students can float their ships. If space permits, let them have races, blowing at their ships to make them go faster.

Name _____

A Ship to Sail

Cut out the two ships, leaving them connected at the top. Glue a floatable object such as a piece of wood or Styrofoam™ between the ships at the bottom. Then glue or tape the front and back of the two ships together and take your ship for a sail.

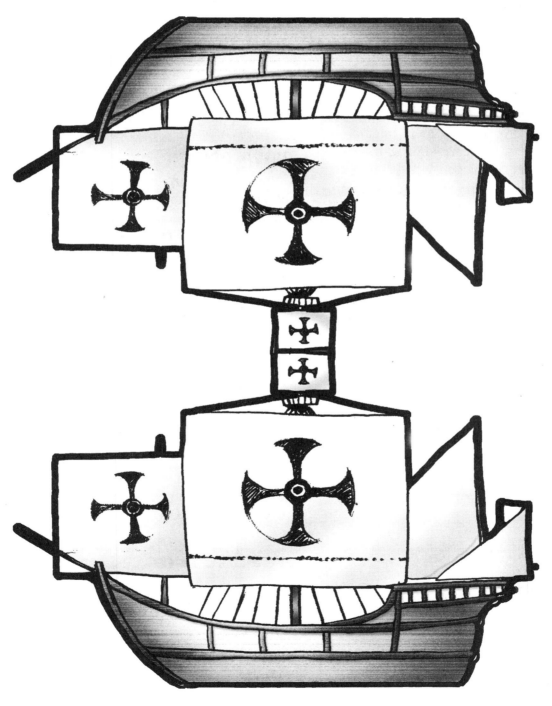

Christopher Columbus

They're Off!

It took three months to get everything and everyone ready to go, but at dawn on August 3, 1492, the small fleet embarked. Columbus, unlike most sea captains of that time, kept a diary or journal of the trip.

The ships had been loaded with enough food to last a year, though Columbus didn't plan on the voyage taking that long. Some of the foods taken along were sea biscuits (hardtack), olive oil, molasses, cheese, honey, raisins, rice, almonds, dried beans, sardines, dried codfish, flour and pickled and salted meats. On calm days the sailors fished and cooked whatever they caught. The meals for the crew were served in a large wooden bowl with no silverware. Everyone used their fingers and often a knife that most sailors carried. The food was usually boiled and the meat was cooked with beans or peas and rice to make stew. Wine and water were provided for drinking.

Columbus wrote in his journal on August 25, 1492 (about three weeks into the voyage), that the *Piñta* had been stopped in the Canary Islands (near Africa, but owned by Spain) for several days to make rudder repairs. A few days later when the repairs were completed, he wrote that they were loading dried meat, salted fish and fruit on the ships before going on their way. They also took aboard more firewood and water.

Map Activity

Have students find the Canary Islands on a world map or globe. Have them note how far Columbus had gone in three weeks and how much farther he had to go.

Eating Like Sailors

Send a note home with students asking that they be allowed to bring a treat for the class. The treat should be food that might have been eaten on Columbus' voyage (fresh fruit, dried fruit, sardines, etc.). List foods that may be brought. Make hard tack by mixing water and flour to form a stiff dough. Flatten bits of dough with your hands to make biscuits. Bake the biscuits on a cookie sheet for 15-20 minutes at 400°F or until slightly brown.

Let students sit on the floor and eat with their fingers. Provide water to drink. Play a tape of ocean sounds for background.

Navigating

Columbus had only four tools to help guide him across the ocean: a compass, a half-hour glass, an astrolabe and a quadrant. The compass was checked against the pole star (North Star). The quadrant was supposed to show the latitude but it was almost impossible to use one accurately in a rolling ship on the ocean. Actually, Columbus seldom navigated by the stars. He used dead reckoning to get where he wanted to go. This was a system of using a compass and the North Star to keep on course. The speed of the ship, the time and the ship's approximate position were written on a chart. Speed was measured by tossing a small, specially designed log over the rail. It was attached to a line that had equally spaced knots tied on it. The number of knots in the line that went over the rail in half a minute gave the speed of the ship. Though we use sophisticated instruments to measure such things today, sea speed still is figured in "knots." It was an inaccurate method and Columbus made many mistakes in the distances he traveled.

Web Site Fun

Let students use computers to visit the Columbus Navigation Homepage web site:
www1.minn.net/~keithp/index.htm

Pictures of Columbus' navigational tools and more information about them is provided.

Christopher Columbus

Compass Calculations

Bring as many compasses to class as you can. If you don't have one for every student, have students work together in pairs or in threes to use a compass. Ask a student who has used a compass before to explain how it works. Then ask them to think about how a compass helped Columbus. What direction was he going? Since a compass always points north, how did it keep Columbus headed in the right direction?

Take your class outside in the playground. Give students various directions to follow such as: take six steps north, then 10 steps west, then three steps south and see where they end up. Let them take turns (individually or in small groups) using their compasses to follow the directions.

Then ask them which directions they need to go to get to certain places (Example: What direction do you need to go to get to the parking lot?) Students use the compasses to figure out the directions they should go.

Trouble on Board

After more than a month at sea, some of the sailors began to get restless. Most of them were not used to sailing without sight of land for many days. There was nothing to see but water and sky all around them. They were sailing fast, covering around 150 miles a day, but nothing seemed to change. Even the wind always blew in the same direction, taking them farther and farther from home and closer to the unknown.

None of the frightening experiences people had warned them about had happened, but according to Columbus' journal, the sight of a falling star upset the sailors.

September 15, 1492: "Early this morning I saw a marvelous meteorite fall in the sea 12 or 15 miles away to the SW. This was taken by some people to be a bad omen, but I calmed them by telling of the numerous occasions that I have witnessed such events. I have to confess that this is the closest that a falling star has ever come to my ship."

No big storms had occurred; the weather was beautiful. Everything was going well. On September 17, Columbus wrote that they saw weeds in the water. The weeds looked like river grass and this was taken to be a sign that they weren't far from land. They were actually entering the Sargasso Sea. Sargasso is seaweed that floats on the water. Birds were sighted and much more grass which made everyone feel they must be near land. But the grass also worried some of the sailors. They were afraid that the grass would become so thick and matted that the ships would get stuck in it and not be able to move. The crew continued to grumble about the wind, too. They were afraid they would never be able to get back home because the wind wouldn't blow them in that direction. In fact, the crew was complaining about almost everything at this point. There was apparently even talk of throwing Columbus overboard some night. Then the captain of the *Pinta* reported that he had seen land! Unfortunately, the next day it was discovered to be just cloud formations.

Columbus sailed on, though calm winds kept him from making his previous speed. He wrote in his journal about seeing porpoises, terns, flying fish and other sea creatures. On October 1, he wrote that he calculated that they had traveled over 2000 miles but he told the pilot they had only come 1752 miles. He was afraid his crew would panic if they knew just how far away from home they were.

Land was finally sighted by a sailor on the *Pinta* on October 11. It was only about six miles away. The next morning Columbus and the other two ship captains went ashore.

Christopher Columbus

Columbus and Crew Rap

Copy the following rap for your students to read to help them understand the different viewpoints Columbus and his crew had about the voyage. Choose one good reader to be Columbus. The rest of the students read the Crew part. Encourage them to read their parts with feeling, appropriate gestures and body language (angry faces, crossed arms, etc.). Columbus should be happy and excited.

Columbus

We've been at sea for just two months
And hasn't it been great?
The weather's fine; the sea is calm.
Good luck will be our fate!

Crew

We've been at sea for two long months
And what has been so great?
We've gone so far we'll never
Get back home. A tragic fate!

Columbus

Last night I saw a wondrous sight—
A brilliant, falling star!
It fell into the sea nearby.
How fortunate we are!

Crew

Last night we saw a fearful sight—
A star fell to the sea!
It must have been a warning
Of the trouble that will be.

Columbus

I saw some grass upon the sea;
I touched it with my hand.
It tells me that we're almost there;
We must be close to land!

Crew

Look at the grass upon the sea.
We're sure it means bad luck.
What if it gets too thick and then
The ship can't move? We're stuck!

Discussion

Ask students to compare Columbus' attitude with his crew's attitude. Did the sailors have good reason for their fears? Did Columbus handle them well? What else could he have done to encourage them?

Point out that part of the problem between Columbus and his crew might have been their differences. Ask students how they were different. (Columbus was Italian; most of the crew was Spanish. Columbus was following a dream; his crew was just doing a job. Columbus had planned and studied for years for the trip and apparently felt no qualms about what might be ahead; the crew had heard wild stories about what might happen to them and the dangers involved in such a trip. And most of the crew had rarely been out of sight of land for long.)

Ask students to share how they think they might have felt if they had been sailors on Columbus' ship.

On Land at Last

The two-month voyage had been amazingly uneventful, but it had seemed long. Now Columbus' dream had come true. He felt his ideas had been proven correct–he had found the East Indies by sailing west! We know, of course, that he had not. Instead of landing off the coast of China or Japan, he was in the Bahama Islands. It was a great accomplishment, but not the one he had planned.

No one knows for sure the exact spot where Columbus went ashore in the Bahamas. There are 35 islands in the Bahamas and 687 cays (coral reefs or sandbars large enough to form small islands). Recent studies done with computers say that Samana Cay south of San Salvador Island was the place. Many scholars disagree. Wherever it was, Columbus claimed it in the name of Spain and named it San Salvador.

Map Activity

Have students find the Bahama Islands on a world map or globe. Have them note how far it is from there to China and Japan.

Christopher Columbus

A New World

After Columbus, as he said, "took possession of the island" in the name of King Ferdinand and Queen Isabella, he met its inhabitants. Somewhat shocked to see that none of the people were wearing clothes of any kind, he described them as tall people with skin the color of sunburnt peasants and pretty eyes. He noted that some of them had painted faces or bodies and they talked a lot, though Columbus could not understand them. He was surprised that the people were not at all the way Marco Polo had described them in his book about his travels in the Orient.

The gentle islanders welcomed the strange looking men peaceably. Columbus gave them small gifts–glass mirrors and beads— and the sailors immediately began trading trinkets with them for parrots and cotton thread and other items. Apparently the islanders were delighted with the simple, unfamiliar gifts. Columbus was excited when he noticed that some of them were wearing gold jewelry. He determined to take at least six of the natives back to Spain to show them off to King Ferdinand and Queen Isabella and to teach them Christianity.

When Columbus and his men explored the island, he was surprised when he didn't see any pagodas with golden roofs as Marco Polo had mentioned. The islanders seemed to live very simply and had few possessions. When he realized that there was no gold on the island, Columbus decided to explore some of the other islands to find gold. For several days he went from one island to another. He described in his journal some of the things he discovered: beautiful trees, fruit, little songbirds, brightly colored fish, whales, lizards, huge flocks of parrots, friendly islanders, even dogs, but no gold.

Discussion

Columbus wrote in his journal that the natives he met would make good servants. Ask students why they think he felt superior to them. Did he really have the right to take possession of their island?

Columbus warned his men that they shouldn't take advantage of the islanders. Some of the sailors were trading the people trinkets worth only pennies for items worth a lot of money. But even he wanted to get as much from them for as little as he could. Was Columbus' treatment of the island people right or wrong? Why?

Let's Trade

Let students experience the art of trading. Send a note home asking parents to let their children bring items for trading to school. These might include pencils, erasers, other inexpensive school materials, small toys, candy, etc. Divide the class into two groups–sailors and islanders. Remind them that they should be fair, but also try to make the best deal they can.

When trading time is over, ask students to tell what they traded and whether or not they think they made a good deal. Point out that while the students knew the value of the items they traded, the island people had no concept of the value of the items Columbus and his men gave them. Is that a fair way to trade? On the other hand, sometimes an item has value to one person but not to another. That's what trading is all about–getting something you value for something you don't value as much. Discuss how this works.

Christopher Columbus

The Search Goes On

As the search for gold continued, many other interesting discoveries were made. One of the best discoveries was the kind of bed many islanders used. Columbus described them as "nets of cotton." They were hammocks and the sailors were delighted with them. They saw how hammocks could make ocean voyages much more comfortable. Instead of sleeping on the hard deck of the ship, a sailor could tie up his hammock and have a good night's sleep swaying with the ship's motion. The next morning, he could simply untie it and roll it up for easy storage.

After exploring several of the islands and cays in the Bahamas and finding no gold, on October 23 Columbus decided to go to the island of Cuba which the natives had told him about. He believed Cuba was actually Japan. When his ship reached Cuba, Columbus and his men began to explore. He was impressed by the natural beauty of the island. They saw a few natives, but they ran away from him and his crew. As they sailed down rivers and gazed at mountains, Columbus imagined finding gold and pearls and taking them back to the king and queen of Spain.

They finally met some island people who wanted to trade with them. These people sent word to other islanders about Columbus. He was becoming convinced that instead of reaching Japan, he was on the mainland of China. He sent some men to walk into the interior to find the city of the Great Khan, the ruler of China. When the search party returned, all they had found was a native village which consisted of 50 huts. There was no Great Khan to be found.

They had, however, found something that was to have a great impact on the world–tobacco. They had seen the islanders roll tobacco leaves into cylinders, stick them in their noses, set them on fire and smoke them! It wasn't long before the habit was adopted by explorers and spread all over Europe.

Columbus decided to sail to yet another island called Bohio, what is today Haiti and the Dominican Republic. But the captain of the *Pinta* had other ideas. Without asking Columbus for permission, Captain Pinzon took his ship toward the north to another island where he hoped to find gold. The *Santa María* and the *Niña* went on to Bohio. The islanders Columbus had on board to take back to Spain were frightened of this island. They told Columbus there were cannibals on Bohio. This did not, however stop him from going ashore. He saw more and more natives wearing gold jewelry, but they were friendly, definitely not cannibals. Columbus believed he was now on the island of Japan and would soon find gold mines.

Columbus' Discoveries

Give a copy of page 19 to each student to complete. Explain that on this first voyage to the Indies, there were some things Columbus wanted to discover that he did not, but he also made some discoveries he hadn't planned on. Students should mark what he found and what he didn't.

Go over students' answers together. Ask students which discoveries were the most important.

Name _____

Columbus' Discoveries

Underline what Columbus hoped to discover on his first voyage across the ocean. Then circle the discoveries he and his crew actually made.

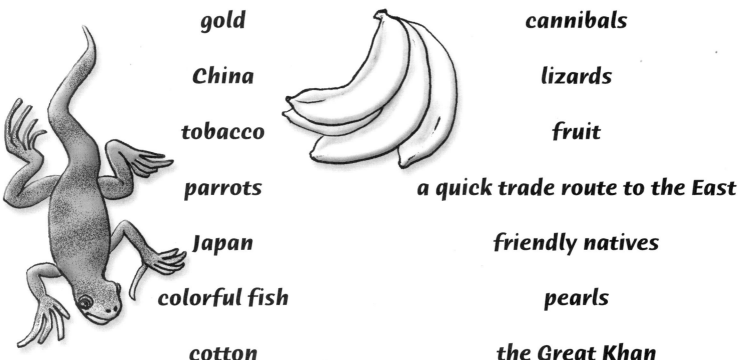

gold

China

tobacco

parrots

Japan

colorful fish

cotton

pagodas with golden roofs

hammocks

mountains

cannibals

lizards

fruit

a quick trade route to the East

friendly natives

pearls

the Great Khan

beautiful trees

whales

new lands no Europeans
knew about

Shipwreck!

On Christmas Eve, Columbus set sail again. He had heard of another place where there was sure to be gold! He hadn't had any sleep for two days because he had been busy entertaining natives. He felt it was important to keep on friendly terms with all of them. That day the ships were tossed about by fierce winds and had to go carefully to avoid the rocks and reefs in the area. But by 11:00 the wind and water was calm and everyone relaxed. Columbus decided to get some much needed sleep, so he went to his cabin and lay down. His second-in-command officer was tired too, so he left the helmsman in charge while he also rested. However, the helmsman was also very tired, so he woke up one of the ship's boys to hold the giant steering wheel while he took a quick nap. This was not unusual. In fact, boys were often given a chance to practice steering a ship late at night when there was no danger. This is probably the way Christopher Columbus had learned many years before.

Columbus had forbidden the practice on this voyage. They were too far from home and there were too many unknown factors to take a chance on something happening. His orders had been disobeyed and trouble lay ahead.

Just after midnight, on Christmas Day, the *Santa María* hit a coral reef. Nobody knew it was there; not even Columbus had suspected it. The ship did not crash into the reef; it simply slid up on the coral so smoothly that it didn't even jar anyone awake. But the boy at the helm knew immediately what had happened when he felt the rudder hit ground. When the boy cried out that the ship had hit a reef, Columbus was the first on deck. He sent men out in a boat to row around the ship to see what damage had been done. But instead of doing what they were told, the sailors began quickly rowing toward the *Niña* so they would be safe. The crew on the *Niña* would not let them come on board, however, and made them return to the *Santa María*. But Columbus' ship was already past saving. The crew of the *Santa María* went on board the *Niña* to wait for morning. Then Columbus sent some men to land to find the island chief and ask for help. The chief brought men in canoes to help Columbus' crew unload the ship before it sank. Everything was saved. Columbus wrote in his journal that "not even a shoestring was lost." It was all stored in a nearby native village.

Now what? Columbus had too many men to take them all on the *Niña* and safely return to Spain. Since the *Pinta* wasn't around to share the load, he would have to leave some men behind. The crew used lumber from the abandoned *Santa María* to build a fortress on the island (Haiti). It was the first European fortress in the New World. During the days when the building was going on, Columbus and the island chief became good friends, and the chief had some of his people help with the building.

When the building was done, the *Niña* left to return to Spain. Two days after they started, the *Pinta* came alongside. Captain Pinzon came aboard the *Niña* and asked Columbus to forgive him for going off on his own. The two ships had to stop for water and supplies for the long trip and to make some repairs to both ships. When they stopped for repairs at another island, they were met by natives attacking them with bows and arrows. When the sailors fought back, the natives ran away. These were the only unfriendly islanders Columbus met. Finally on January 16, the two ships headed for Spain.

Christopher Columbus

Pickin' Up the Pieces Relay

To prepare for this game you'll need to gather a variety of objects to represent pieces from the wrecked ship that students will be picking up and bringing to shore (small boards, magazines, canned food, shoes, clothes, boxes, etc.). Stick a label on each item to tell what it represents (ship's rail, food, map, supplies, clothing, etc.). Place all the items in a big pile at a certain place in the playground or gym. Then print on a slip of paper an item in the pile and a method of traveling in the water (swim, float, canoe or rowboat). Make a slip for each item in the pile (at least one for each student). Put all the slips of paper in a paper bag. Use masking tape to make a starting line or use a sidewalk for that purpose.

To play the game, divide students into two teams: sailors and natives. Explain that the two teams will be racing to see who can bring back the most pieces of the wrecked ship first. The two teams line up and the first person on each team chooses a slip of paper from the bag. The paper tells the student what he or she must find in the pile and bring back as well as how he or she must move back from the pile.

If the slip chosen says "swim," the student must figure out a way to carry the item back while moving both arms in a swimming motion. If the item is small, the student can clutch it in a hand while swimming, but if it is too large to hold that way, the student must figure out another way to carry it.

If the slip says "float," the student may pick up the item and hurry back to the starting line *backwards* as if floating on his or her back.

If the slip says "canoe," the student must use both hands to pretend to paddle a canoe while carrying the item (perhaps between the legs or under the chin since both hands must be used to paddle).

If the slip says "rowboat," the student must use both hands as if rowing with two oars in a boat going backwards toward the starting line with the item held between the legs, under the chin or however it can be carried.

Make sure students choose and read their directions *before* leaving the starting line to run to the shipwreck pile. When all the items in the pile have been brought to shore, the team with the most items wins the game.

Another Shipwreck Story

There are many interesting and exciting books about shipwrecks. One of the best is *The Swiss Family Robinson*. Read selections from this book to your students. The account of how the family retrieved so many useful items from the wrecked ship is an especially good chapter to read at this point in the study of Columbus. After you read it, ask students how Columbus' experience compared to the book.

If time permits, play the Disney video of *The Swiss Family Robinson* for your students. Then talk about how it compares with Columbus' story.

See page 5 for more information about this book and video.

Homeward Bound

After being in what he thought was the East Indies for about four months, Columbus was homeward bound, leaving behind one wrecked ship and 39 of his crew. He had taken careful note of the trade winds that had helped them sail west so easily, and he knew he had to avoid them on his way back to Spain. He wasn't sure where the tradewinds began, but his plan was to sail diagonally across them, then sail north, then east. He never worried that he wouldn't be able to find his way home. So with careful calculating and a lot of guess-work, they set off across the wide ocean.

The return voyage was peaceful at first, but on February 13, 1493, Columbus wrote in his journal that the wind "increased and the sea became terrible, with the waves crossing each other and pounding the ships." The weather continued to be bad for the next two days. To make matters worse, the *Pinta* and the *Santa María* lost sight of each other. Columbus began to worry that if something happened to his ship no one would ever know of his discoveries. He wrote it all down on a piece of parchment (incorrectly of course), wrapped the parchment in cloth, covered it with wax, put it in a barrel and threw the barrel overboard (somewhat like sailors or stranded people put messages in bottles and throw them in the sea to hopefully find their way to civilization).

As far as we know, nobody ever found the message in the barrel. However, six days later the *Niña* found its way to an island. Columbus was sure it was one of the Azores. He sent some men ashore to see where they were, and they were told that it was the island of Santa Maria, the farthest island east in the Azores, Portuguese land.

Map Activity

Have students find the Azores on a world map or globe. Have them note how close they are to Portugal and to Spain, then how far from the Bahamas. How far from home was Columbus? Which took longer, Columbus' trip west or the return trip?

Navigating by Dead Reckoning

Some people have said that Columbus sailing across the ocean, then returning and ending up so close to home was like finding a needle in a haystack. Let students try to find their way around by dead reckoning.

Tell a student to make his or her way across the room or playground to a specific point. Let the student use a compass to determine which direction to go to get to the place. Then blindfold the student and turn him or her around three times. The only help the student gets is from another student with a compass who can tell the blindfolded student which direction he or she is facing. The blindfolded student must try to reach the goal, only asking what direction he or she is heading.

Emphasize to students that speed is not important in this game, but accuracy is. The blindfolded student must use his or her mind to figure out which way to move. Demonstrate how the student should adjust depending on the compass information he or she is given. For example: The student determines that the goal is directly west of the starting point. He or she is facing east, so the student turns halfway around to face west and begins to walk. After several steps the student asks the direction and is told he or she is going northwest, so the student turns slightly to the left and continues walking. After more steps, when the student is told he or she is headed southwest, a slight turn to the right should help the student end up near the goal.

Let every student have a chance to try out his or her navigational skills this way.

Christopher Columbus

Almost Home

Unknown to Columbus, the king of Portugal had sent word to all the islands under his rule that Christopher Columbus should be stopped if he was located. When the men he had sent ashore did not come back, Columbus knew something was up. The Portuguese captain of the island sent word that he wanted the sailors to stay ashore with him to tell him their stories of discovery. Columbus agreed, but did not go ashore. The next day more sailors asked permission to go ashore to a religious shrine to thank God for safety on the voyage. Columbus allowed them to go. The men were captured by villagers and the captain of the island. When the men did not return to the ship, Columbus didn't know if they had been kidnapped or if their boat had been wrecked.

Later the captain of the island and several armed men rowed out to the ship to take Columbus ashore, but Columbus wouldn't go. He told the captain of the island that he had letters of recommendation from the king and queen of Spain, but the captain would not come on the ship to look at the papers. He returned to shore.

When a storm came up, Columbus had to take his ship out to sea to deeper water. When the storm was over, he sailed back into the harbor. Two priests and the captain's secretary came out to the ship and asked to see the letters Columbus had. After looking at them carefully, the three men left and Columbus' crew was soon released.

As soon as the weather allowed it, Columbus sailed away. However, new storms hit. One was so bad it split the ship's sails and the wind and waves were so fierce, the crew thought they would be drowned. But the ship and everyone on it survived the storm and the next morning they saw that they had been blown close to the harbor of Lisbon, Portugal. They sailed into the harbor and were met by a Portuguese warship.

The master of the warship came to Columbus' ship in a smaller armed boat and ordered Columbus to get aboard. Columbus refused. He showed his letters from the king and queen of Spain to him. The man took the letters to show to his captain. When the captain read the letters, he came with great ceremony and offered to help Columbus in whatever way he could. Columbus still did not go ashore, but many Portuguese people came aboard his ship to congratulate him on his successful voyage.

Then King John of Portugal sent a letter inviting Columbus to come and see him. The king also ordered his agents to give Columbus and his crew anything they needed without charge and do for them anything they wanted. Apparently the king had changed his mind about Columbus! Though he did not really want to go and see the king, Columbus went to avoid suspicion. He wrote about his visit with the king: "He indicated that he was greatly pleased that the voyage had been accomplished successfully." When Columbus left, the king gave him some messages for the king and queen of Spain and showed him great kindness.

Discussion

Talk about the king's about-face. Why do you think the King of Portugal changed from wanting to capture Columbus to honoring him and being kind to him?

Do you think the king was jealous of Columbus? Why?

Christopher Columbus

Honored in Spain

It must have been frustrating for Columbus to have been delayed for so many days in the Azores and then in Portugal. He was so close to home, but because of the king of Portugal it took Columbus three weeks to cover the last short distance to Spain. Finally on March 13, 1493, he set sail for Spain. Two days later the *Niña* sailed into the harbor at Palos, Spain, about seven and a half months after it had left there. Amazingly, the *Pinta* arrived later that same day. The ship had survived the storms and made it home after being separated from the *Niña* for most of the return voyage.

Parties and banquets were given all over the city for the returning sailors. They had conquered the great unknown; they had crossed the great Western Sea and were now celebrities. Columbus went to Barcelona, taking the six islanders with him, to see King Ferdinand and Queen Isabella. He also took a detailed paper he had written on how the islands he had discovered should be colonized. He wanted to take 2000 people immediately to set up villages and farms in the New World.

On the way to Barcelona, almost every town he went through had a welcoming parade for Columbus and his party. The king and queen had ordered banners hung in the city and their royal court came out to escort him. Columbus was a hero! Everyone wanted to meet him and talk with him. Perhaps he remembered with a smile two years before when many of these people had laughed at his ideas.

Columbus spent hours with the king and queen. They listened spellbound as he told of his adventures and discoveries. They examined the items he had brought back and met the island natives. They talked about sending another expedition immediately, larger this time. Columbus could have anything he wanted! He stayed in the royal household and went riding with the king. It was the high point of his life.

A Coat of Arms

About two months after Columbus' meeting with them, the king and queen gave Columbus the right to have his own coat of arms. The one he was assigned had a castle and a lion on it. A few years later he added other symbols as a reminder of his adventures.

Make a copy of Columbus' coat of arms on page 25 and give one to each student. Study it together. Ask them to identify the symbols on the shield, then guess why Columbus added the bottom two (islands and five anchors).

Discuss what students would want on their coats of arms if they had them. Remind them that the symbols should be reminders of significant events in their lives or of personal characteristics. For example, a student who is a sports enthusiast might include a sports symbol such as a ball and bat or baseball glove, ice skates or a soccer ball on his or her coat of arms. A student who is known for courage might include a lion as on Columbus' coat of arms.

Hand out copies of the coat of arms shield on page 26. Challenge each student to design his or her own coat of arms. Encourage them to sketch their ideas in pencil on another sheet of paper first until they have the design just the way they want it. Then they can pencil it in on the shield and color it with markers or crayons.

When the students are done, mount the coats of arms on the walls around the room for everyone to enjoy before they are taken home.

Name _____

Columbus' Coat of Arms

Name _____

My Coat of Arms

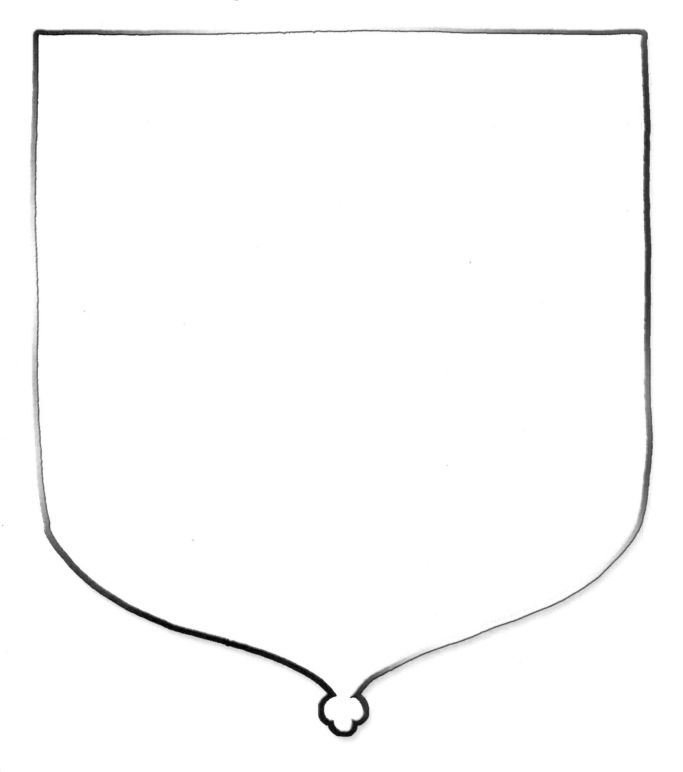

Christopher Columbus

Loading Up

About six months later Columbus took off again for the New World he had discovered. King Ferdinand and Queen Isabella were anxious for him to go back as quickly as possible and begin to colonize the islands before Portugal beat them to it. However, this expedition was much bigger than the first, and it took longer to get everything ready. There were 17 ships to carry about 1400 people: soldiers and horses, farmers, craftsmen, laborers and priests. Everyone was excited about this trip. Almost 200 men paid their own way to go on the voyage for the adventure and probably hoping to find gold.

Enough supplies for two years were loaded aboard the ships as well as chickens, cattle, donkeys, sheep, goats, pigs and seeds to plant. Since no one had ever attempted a colonizing enterprise like this before, every possibility had to be thought of and planned for.

What Should We Take?

Divide students into small groups of about four or five. Have students imagine they're traveling with Columbus to a new world to live. Challenge them to decide what they need to take with them. Have each group make a list of the items they decide to take. Then have the groups share their lists aloud to see how they compare.

The Second Voyage

Finally, everything was ready. On September 25, 1493, Columbus sailed off at the head of the fleet in a ship he again called the *Santa María*. It was an easy voyage that took less than a month. The first islands they visited were quite a bit south of where he had landed on the original voyage. They sailed among many new islands until they reached Haiti (named Hispaniola by Columbus on his first trip) where Columbus had left part of his crew in a hastily built fortress.

All the men left behind were dead and the fortress had been burned down. The native islanders told Columbus that some of the men had been killed by disease, some had fought among themselves and killed one another and the rest had been killed by raiding parties of natives from other islands. Columbus suspected that the islanders of Haiti had killed the sailors themselves, but he could not prove it. It is a mystery that will probably never be solved.

After a few days Columbus led his fleet east to search for a safer place to build a new colony and, hopefully, find gold. Strong winds caused many of the passengers and Columbus to be sick during the two-week trip. When they found what seemed to be a good island for settlement, they went ashore and began building houses and fortifications though many of them were still sick.

A search party sent to look for gold found some, but not as much as Columbus had hoped. About a month later he sent most of his ships back to Spain for more supplies. The settlers were unhappy and Columbus was not very successful in keeping peace and order. Soon he set sail to look for gold on other islands. After two months of exploring and not finding any gold Columbus, now sick, returned to the settlement. It took several months for him to recover.

Plus or Minus?

Give each student a copy of page 28. Have them decide what they would have liked about living in the new world settlement and what they would not have liked. Compare answers and discuss them.

Name _____

Plus or Minus?

Listed below are some of the new and different things the settlers in the New World had to face. Make a plus sign next to each one you think you would have liked and a minus sign next to what you wouldn't have liked.

___ **Building your own house**

___ **Getting to know friendly (?) natives**

___ **Eating fresh fruits and vegetables**

___ **Searching for gold**

___ **Being far from home**

___ **No school**

___ **Eating iguana (lizard)**

___ **Making your own clothes**

___ **Working hard**

___ **Hot temperatures**

___ **Eating paca (a large rat)**

___ **Mosquitoes**

___ **Nowhere to go except to unsettled islands**

___ **Learning the islanders' language to communicate with them**

___ **Counting on ships from Spain for all of your supplies**

___ **Fishing**

___ **Hunting animals for food**

___ **Strange birds, plants and animals**

___ **Learning a new way of life**

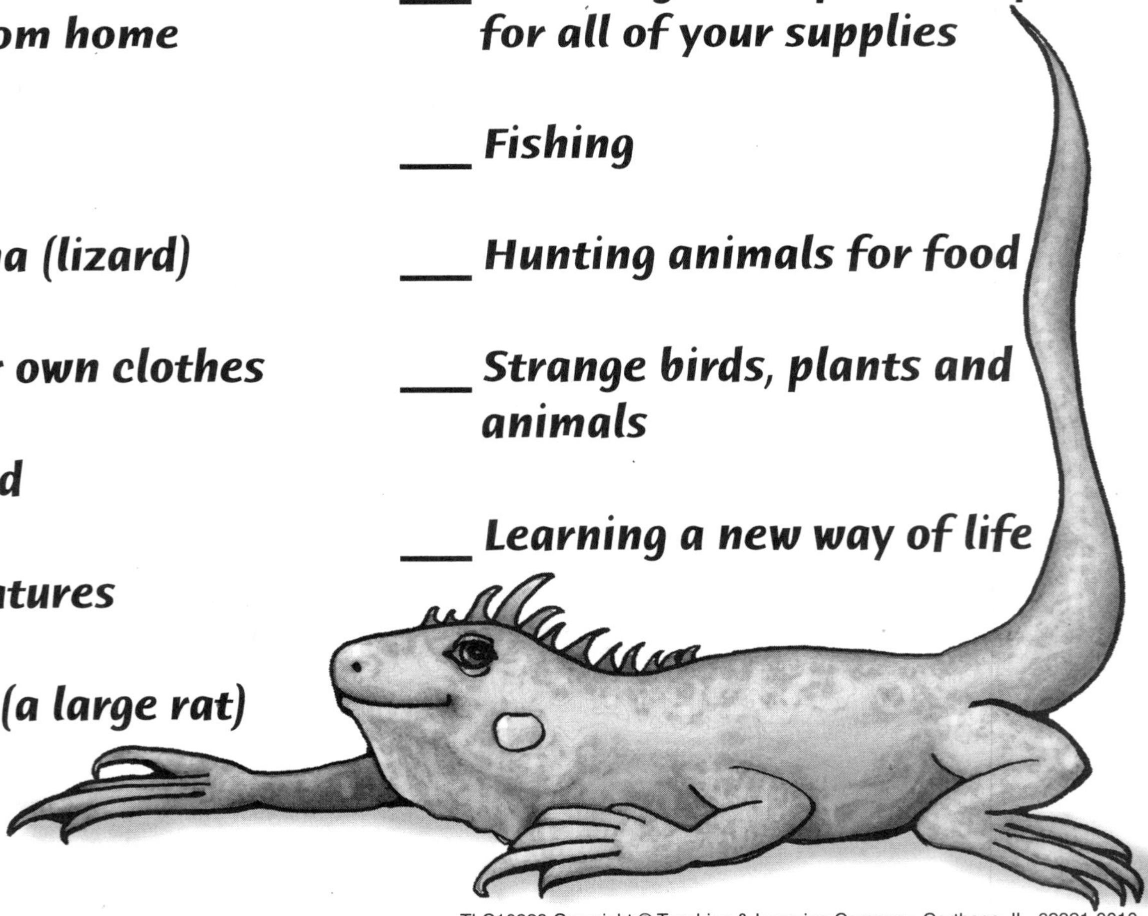

Christopher Columbus

A Voyage Over and Another Begun

Columbus didn't really want to return to Spain since he didn't have much gold to show the king and queen, he had not found Asia and the colony was not as well controlled as he would have liked. But he couldn't put it off any longer.

His return to Spain was not the cause for big celebration as his first had been. Some who had traveled with him on his second voyage complained about the way he governed the new colony, and passengers on supply ships going back and forth to the new colony reported that things were not going well there. But King Ferdinand and Queen Isabella received Columbus warmly and were anxious to hear about his latest adventure. They gave him the ships he asked for to sail back to the New World and make further discoveries.

On his third voyage Columbus was sick for most of the trip. He sailed farther south and discovered a new island which he named Trinidad. Then he discovered what he thought was a new island. He soon realized it was a new continent–known today as South America. He was thrilled. He still had not found Asia as he had hoped, but he had found a continent that was not on any charts or maps.

Map Activity

Have students locate the island of Trinidad on a world map or globe, then South America. Have them note how far south these places are from where Columbus sailed on his first voyage.

Trouble in Paradise

During Columbus' absence, many settlers in the new world colony had died from sickness and many more were very sick. The relationship between the settlers and the island natives had become hostile since the settlers badly exploited the natives, trying to turn them into slaves. A representative of the king and queen, sent to the island to take care of the problems, sent Columbus back to Spain in chains to stand trial for mismanagement. Instead of being welcomed back and praised for discovering a new continent, he was handed over for trial.

The king and queen still liked Columbus, so he was met with great courtesy at the court. The charges against him were dropped and all but one of his rights and privileges were restored to him. He was no longer the governor of the islands he had discovered.

Familiar Words

Explain that the languages spoken by the natives on the islands Columbus explored were not written down, but the men with him wrote down many of the unfamiliar words they heard. Today some of these words are an everyday part of our vocabulary.

Give each student a copy of page 30 to test their understanding of these words "borrowed" from the islanders of the New World.

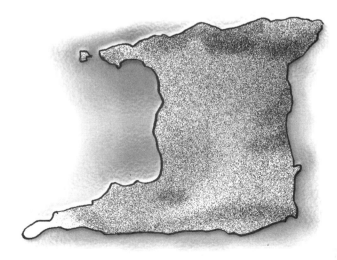

Name _____

Familiar Words

Read the following familiar words which we "borrowed" from the islanders Columbus discovered. Draw a line from each word to the picture it matches.

barbecue

canoe

tobacco

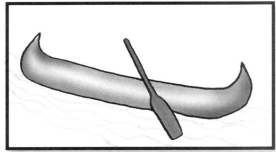

hammock

hurricane

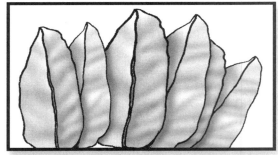

iguana

manatee

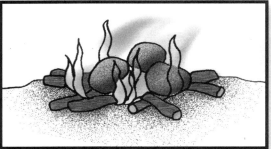

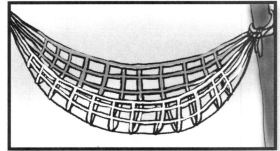

maize

Columbus' Final Voyage

Columbus was allowed to go on a fourth voyage to the New World, taking his younger son Ferdinand with him this time. Columbus was sick for much of the voyage and though he hoped to find a passage through the islands to Asia, he found Central America instead. He was convinced that it was Asia. The farther south they traveled, the more gold they saw. Columbus sent men ashore to ask the natives about their gold. The men were told there was gold everywhere. When they came back to the ship, every man had some gold.

Columbus had log cabins built to found a colony. He chose 80 men to stay behind. Then he heard that the natives planned to burn down the new settlement. To keep this from happening, Columbus sent men to capture the native leader, but he escaped. Later when Columbus sent men ashore to gather wood and water for the return voyage to Spain, natives attacked them. Many of Columbus' men were killed and others badly wounded. The survivors returned to their ships and sailed away. Before long their ships were leaking and so badly in need of repair, one was abandoned to sink. Columbus made it to the island of Jamaica but was stranded there.

Many of his crew mutinied and went ashore. They caused problems with the islanders which made the islanders refuse to provide Columbus with food or water. But he knew by reading his almanac that an eclipse of the moon was due to occur in three days. He warned the islanders that if they refused to help him, he would pray to his God to make the moon disappear. When the eclipse occurred right on schedule, the islanders panicked. They promised to do anything Columbus wanted if he would just make the moon return. Of course, the eclipse ended and after that he had no more problems with the islanders.

After being marooned on Jamaica for more than a year, Columbus and his crew were rescued. Two and a half months later Columbus sailed for Spain. No one even noticed his return this time. Shortly after his return, Columbus' friend and main supporter, Queen Isabella,

died. When he asked King Ferdinand to provide ships for a fifth voyage to the New World, the king refused. Columbus had been sick for some time, and on May 20, 1506, he died.

Though he never accomplished what he had intended, Christopher Columbus had made great discoveries and opened the way for others to the New World. He helped change the course of world history.

Discussion

How did Columbus' voyages compare to space exploration in this century? Which do you think took more courage, sailing across the ocean to an unknown destination or going to the moon? Why?

How would your life be different today if Columbus had never had the courage to cross the ocean?

Action Rhyme/Skit

Copy page 32 for each student. Assign parts and provide simple, appropriate costumes such as robes, crowns, sailor hats, etc., and props such as coins wrapped in gold paper or foil and a small telescope. Students may read their parts as an action rhyme or put a little more interaction in them for a skit.

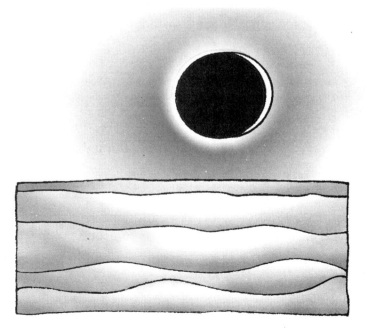

Columbus' Great Adventure

Action Rhyme/Skit

Characters

Trader, Columbus, King of Portugal, Narrator, King Ferdinand, Queen Isabella, Sailors, Natives, Townspeople

Trader

(Pacing the floor with arms outspread)
I've spent my life trading from the East to the West,
Bringing spices and gold and silks; all the best!
But the Turks have cut off trade all around.
We must go east by ship: a sea route must be found!

Columbus

(Looking out across the ocean)
Since I was a boy I've loved the sea,
Sailing anywhere is the most fun to me.
Now the goal of my life is to find a way
To sail to the east without delay.

Columbus

(Facing the King of Portugal)
King John, I believe if I should sail west
I'd find the East Indies before all the rest!
If Portugal sends me, I'll bring back treasure
And fame for you, Oh King, without measure.

King of Portugal

(Facing Columbus, laughing)
Columbus, you're crazy! Really you are.
You're just a dreamer; you'll never go far.
We'll get to the east without help from you!
Now leave, for your time with me is through.

Narrator

(As Columbus walks away)
Columbus was down, but he wasn't done.
Maybe in Spain he'd get help from someone.

Columbus

(Kneeling before King Ferdinand and Queen Isabella)
Oh King, oh Queen, if you'll sponsor my trip,
I'll go west to the East Indies in a ship.
I'll make great discoveries and bring back much gold.
For the East has great riches; that's what I've been told.

King Ferdinand & Queen Isabella

Columbus, your dream is a great one we know.
We'll provide what you want so you can go.
We'll anxiously wait for your return.
There's so much of the east that we want to learn.

Sailors

(Swaying back and forth as if on a ship)
Captain Columbus says we'll find the east,
But it seems we've been sailing for six months at least!
Could he be wrong? Does he really know?
Will we all die? Wait–what's that? Land ho!

Natives

(Welcoming sailors and Columbus)
Who are these people with the strange-looking clothes?
Did they come from the sky? Nobody knows!
We try to help them, but they don't understand.
And why are they saying our home is their land?

Columbus

(Looking proud)
Our voyage was successful! We crossed the Great Sea
And found the East Indies, thanks mostly to me.
I lost a ship and left some of my men,
But I'll pick them up when I come back again.

Townspeople

(Lining up and waving as Columbus passes by)
Welcome home, Hero! You did what you said.
We thought by this time you all might be dead.
You conquered the ocean and you did it your way.
A cheer for Columbus–Hip! Hip! Hooray!